CONTENTS

KU-421-417

All about rainforests

Rainforests are the lush green jungles of the world. They provide a home for more species of animals and plants than any other habitat on Earth.

Rainforests cover about 6% of the world's surface, but that figure is going down all the time. It is estimated that every minute about 2,000 rainforest trees are destroyed. That adds up to hundreds of millions of trees disappearing every year. In this book you can find out all about rainforests and what's being done to prevent their destruction.

What is a rainforest?

Rainforests are vast forests where it rains nearly every day and the temperature is always warm. This warmth and moisture make them ideal places for plants to grow.

From the sky, a rainforest looks like a huge green mass of broccoli tops, and all the trees look much the same. In fact there are many hundreds of different kinds of trees growing side by side. Each large tree is home to many smaller plants that trail themselves over its branches.

Standing in a rainforest

If you visited a tropical rainforest you would find it a hot and steamy place. Your clothes would soon be damp, especially if you

From above, the rainforest looks like a mass of trees that are all the same. In fact, there are many different kinds of tree.

got caught in one of the daily showers of rain. The air would smell mouldy because the ground is covered with rotting leaves. It would be quite dark and gloomy, too, since hardly any sunlight penetrates through the thick layers of foliage.

You would probably hear the screeches and calls of all kinds of wild animals above your head. More than half of all the known animal species in the world live in rainforests. Most of them live above ground, among the tree branches, where they can find food and shelter.

WHEN TREES DISAPPEAR

Rainforests are being destroyed by humans. People cut down the trees to sell the wood, to clear the land for farming, or to use it for mining, oil-drilling, dams and roads.

When the trees go, so do the homes of huge numbers of animals and plants. We could even be losing plants that might have provided us with powerful medicines against our worst

diseases (see p 20). The destruction of the rainforests may also be contributing to world climate change, with serious results for everyone (see p 8).

For these reasons international efforts are being made by both scientists and politicians to stop the destruction. You can find out what you can do to help at the end of this book.

Workers use a bulldozer to clear part of an Indonesian rainforest.

Where to find rainforests

Most rainforests grow around the Equator, in an area that stretches around the middle of the Earth. Here, day and night are of equal length and the Sun's heat is fierce all year long. The temperature is always hot and rain falls regularly.

Jungles in this region are called equatorial rainforests. There are a few rainforests further away from the Equator, in areas of Australasia and North America. These are called temperate rainforests. They have lots of rainfall but not year-round warmth.

South and Central America
The world's biggest equatorial rainforest grows around the Amazon, one of the world's largest rivers. The forest stretches all the way across the middle of South America; a fifth of all the world's known plants and animals live there.

Central America was once completely covered in rainforest too, but more than half of it has been cleared over the years to make way for plantations and cattle pastures.

Asia
Asia's equatorial rainforests stretch from India and Myanmar in the west to Malaysia in the east. They include the jungle-covered islands of Java and Borneo. In parts of south-east Asia it is hot and humid all year round but on mainland Asia there is a monsoon climate. This means that torrential rains fall at certain times of the year. This rainy season is followed by a drier season.

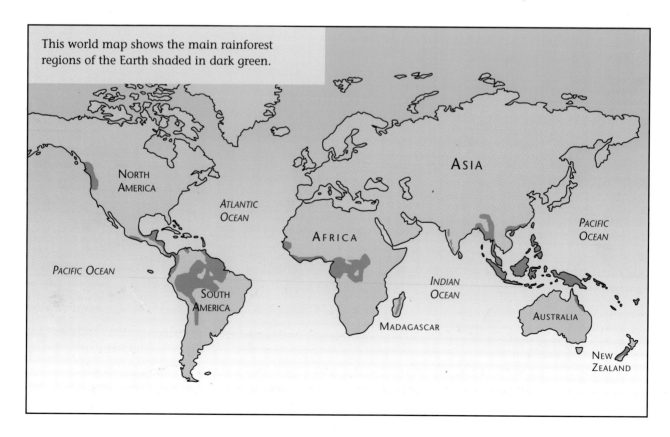

This world map shows the main rainforest regions of the Earth shaded in dark green.

The world's second-largest rainforest region is situated in Central Africa. Here there are several different kinds of rainforest, including mangrove swamps and cloud forests.

Mangrove swamps are a type of rainforest that grows in coastal areas, where the water is salty. The mangrove trees stand high on their roots, which act like stilts. The roots suck up the water but filter out the harmful salt.

Cloud forests grow in high places such as mountains. These forests are misty and the trees obtain most of the moisture they need from mist rather than from rain. Gorillas, the world's biggest apes, live in the African cloud forests of Uganda.

Off the south-east coast of Africa, the island of Madagascar is home to many unique rainforest plants and animals, including lemurs. But 90% of its forest has now gone and the rest is in danger of disappearing in the next 20 years.

A mangrove swamp in West Africa. African rainforests are remote places that are difficult to visit and study.

Asia's rainforests are home to some of the world's most endangered mammals, such as the orang-utan and the tiger. Fossil records show that these jungles have existed for up to 100 million years, but a third of them have disappeared since 1960. They are being rapidly cleared to create farmed plantations for crops such as oil palms.

Australasia

In parts of Australia, New Zealand and Papua New Guinea rain blows in from the Pacific Ocean. This helps create temperate rainforests that contain wildlife found nowhere else on the planet. Unusual creatures, such as the rainforest possum and the duck-billed platypus, thrive here.

Rainforest science

Important natural processes happen in the rainforest to keep the trees alive. Although these processes cannot be seen they are vital, and when they stop there are serious consequences.

Water recycling

Rainforest trees recycle the rain that falls on them. An amazing 4 to 8 m (13 to 20 ft) of rain falls on rainforests every year. Some of this falls on the leaves of the trees; the roots soak up any that falls to the ground. The moisture travels up the tree trunks to the leaves and from there it gets slowly released into the air by evaporation. Half of all the rain that falls on the Amazon rainforest returns to the sky this way. The water vapour gradually rises up into the air and forms rainclouds, which later drop their rain nearby. In the Amazon it rains heavily three or four times a week, and there are regular short thunderstorms as well.

Photosynthesis

The billions of leaves in the rainforest soak up sunlight like tiny solar panels. They also take in a gas called carbon dioxide, or CO_2, from the air. They use the light energy and the CO_2 to make nutrients, which help the trees to grow. When they do this they also release the gas, oxygen, into the air. This whole process is called photosynthesis. So much of it happens in the rainforests that they have been called "the lungs of the world".

Cycling nutrients

Trees need chemicals called nutrients to help them grow healthily. Rainforest soil is very low in nutrients because the large amounts of rain washed them away long ago. However, trees have their own way of creating a supply: when leaves fall to the ground they rot, putting nutrients back into the soil. The trees then absorb these through their roots.

CHANGING THE WEATHER?

When areas of rainforest are cut down, water recycling stops happening. This may change the local climate. The water vapour stops making rainclouds, and instead of getting the regular rain they are used to, people living in nearby areas might find there isn't enough rain for them to grow their crops.

Burning rainforest wood could be affecting the climate of our entire world. When fuel is burnt, the gas CO_2 is released. Scientists believe that too much of this gas in the world's atmosphere causes global warming.

We all need the protective blanket of gases called the atmosphere to create an environment where we can all thrive. Too much carbon dioxide in that blanket, however, prevents enough of the Sun's heat from escaping into space.

Scientists have noticed that the Earth's climate is warming up very quickly, a process they call global warming. Eventually the North and South Poles may melt and cause rises in sea levels. To prevent this happening we need to limit the amount of CO_2 we create. Cars, factories and power plants produce a lot, but it's also estimated that at least one-fifth of the world's excess CO_2 is coming from the burning of rainforest wood.

In the rainforest rain usually falls in short and heavy bursts.

Rainforest layers

A rainforest tree is like a natural version of a block of flats: different creatures and plants live on different levels. Trees rely on animals to spread pollen and seeds. Animals rely on the trees to provide food, such as juicy fruits and sugary nectar.

Overstorey

The very top of the rainforest is called the overstorey. Rainforest trees usually grow to around 50 m (164 ft) in height, but some trees stretch high above the others, up to 60 m (197 ft). They are called "emergent" trees.

Large birds such as harpy eagles sometimes use emergent trees as nesting sites and lookout positions. They make a good place for birds of prey to spot their quarry in the branches below.

Canopy

Beneath the overstorey there is a dense layer of leaves and branches called the canopy. It's the busiest section of the forest. Birds, small mammals, reptiles, frogs and insects all live here because it has a rich store of fruit, flower nectar and seeds to eat. In an equatorial rainforest there are no seasons, such as autumn or spring. Instead, each tree species flowers and fruits at its own particular time.

Understorey

The understorey is the area below the canopy, where the leaves and branches aren't so dense. But there is still a large amount of wildlife. Parrots fly around and monkeys can sometimes be seen swinging from rope-like plants called lianas. Lianas look as if they are hanging down from above, but in fact they grow up from the ground.

An emergent tree is taller than the others in the forest. It makes a good perch for birds of prey.

DOWN BELOW

Underneath rainforest trees there is a layer of plant material called "leaf litter". In time, micro-organisms and fungi rot the leaf litter, and this process replenishes essential nutrients in the soil (see p 8). If you turned over some leaf litter you might spot beetles, ants or centipedes, because many insects live here. In contrast to these tiny creatures, some of the largest rainforest mammals also roam between the trees on the forest floor. In the Amazon, for example, large pig-like creatures called tapirs snuffle around looking for food.

Many insects live in the rainforest. These leafcutter ants make their home in the damp layer of leaf litter on the rainforest floor.

Shrub layer

At ground level in undisturbed areas, called "primary" forest, there is little sunlight so the vegetation is usually quite sparse. Baby trees and bushes grow here.

Forest that has been thinned out by fire or by humans is called "secondary" forest. Here more sunlight can penetrate to the shrub layer and it tends to be more crowded, with different types of plants. It's harder to walk through the shrub layer in a secondary forest.

In the shrub layer giant buttress roots splay out around trees to keep them standing up. These thick roots make a booming sound when they are kicked. In Amazonia local people signal to each other by drumming on them.

Rainforest animals

Over 50% of the world's animal species live in the rainforests, and that's only counting the ones we know about! If you visited, you'd hear animals screeching, calling and trilling, especially at night when many of the rainforest creatures are active.

Reptiles

The rainforest makes an ideal home for snakes and lizards because it is a warm climate and there is lots of food around. Tree snakes coil their way around the branches looking for small creatures to eat. Lizards sit waiting to catch passing insects.

Some rainforest snakes are deadly poisonous to humans, or large enough to crush someone to death. For instance, the world's heaviest snake, the anaconda, lives in the Amazon region. It can grow up to 9 m (30 ft) long and as thick as a human body.

Frogs

Much of the night-time noise in a rainforest comes from tiny frogs calling to each other up in the forest canopy. They have sticky pads on their toes to help them climb. Many of them live in small pools of water that collect in bowl-shaped plants growing high in the trees.

Rainforest frogs are often brightly coloured, to warn other animals that they are poisonous to eat. The strongest poison produced by any animal in the world comes from the tiny poison arrow frog, which is no bigger than a human thumbnail.

Mammals

Rainforest mammals range from tiny bats to big gorillas and tigers, and 90% of all the world's monkeys live in rainforests. There are many species of rodent, too, including the Amazonian capybara – the world's biggest – which can grow to the size of an adult sheep.

A red-eyed tree frog in Panama, Central America. Rainforest frogs are often brightly coloured. They make lots of noise when they call to each other at night.

THE MORE THE BETTER

We may be losing 50 animal and plant species every day because of the destruction of the rainforests. This could cause serious problems in the future. Scientists believe it is very important that our planet has "biodiversity", which means it has as many different animal and plant species as possible to help keep all life healthy and thriving. Less species could mean that, over time, more diseases and harmful genetic defects could spread through the animal and plant kingdoms.

Birds

Roughly 30% of the world's birds live in rainforests. Vividly coloured macaws and hornbills use their tough beaks to feed off a rich harvest of fruit and nuts in the trees. Tiny birds, including hummingbirds no bigger than bees, rely on flower nectar for nourishment.

Insects and spiders

There are probably many rainforest insects still to discover. Some scientists think that up to 90% of the world's insects may live in rainforest regions. They range from giant beetles the size of a human hand and moths the size of dinner plates to tiny ants that you would need a magnifying glass to see properly. Scientists estimate that one rainforest tree provides a home for up to 200 different insect types. The number of actual insects per tree probably runs into many hundreds of thousands.

Rainforest trees contain a wide range of spiders, too, ranging from aggressive hunting spiders to thousands of small spiders living together in colonies in giant webs.

This brilliantly coloured blue Morpho butterfly lives in South American rainforests.

Rainforest plants

Rainforest plants vary in size from the world's biggest flowers to microscopic plants too small to see with the naked eye. They provide us with all kinds of food, flavourings, medicines and other useful products, such as rubber.

Plants we use

Bananas, peppers, okra, peanuts and cashews are some of the familiar food plants that are grown in rainforest regions. Coffee and tea, oil palms, vanilla, sugar and all kinds of spices are farmed there, too.

Tropical forest oils and gums are used in insecticides, rubber products, paint, varnish, cosmetics and shampoos.

Most importantly, rainforest plant extracts are used in many modern medicines. For instance, 2,000 tropical forest plants have been shown to be helpful in treating cancer. So far scientists have only tested one in ten

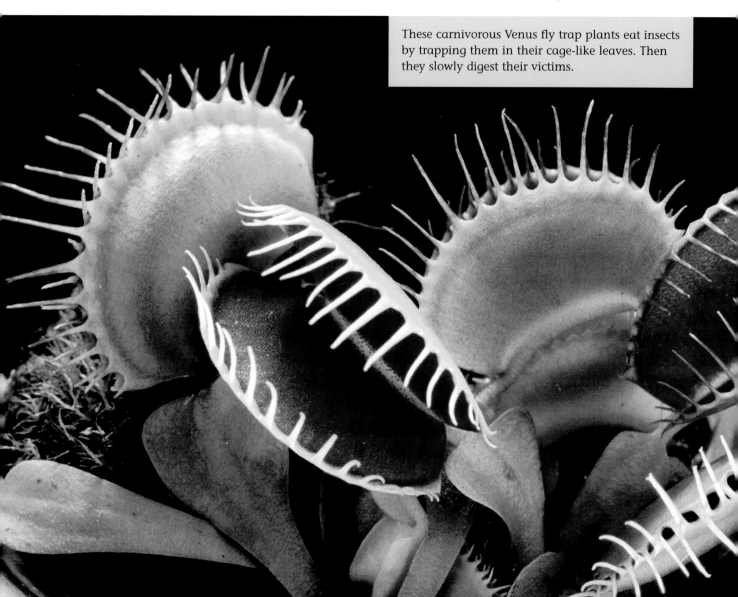

These carnivorous Venus fly trap plants eat insects by trapping them in their cage-like leaves. Then they slowly digest their victims.

of the rainforest plants they know about (see p 21). There could be many more beneficial plants that could disappear before scientists ever get the chance to investigate their properties.

Killer plants

Some rainforest plants are carnivorous, which means they eat meat. They trap small creatures and then digest them to absorb nutrients. Some large carnivorous plants will even trap and eat small mammals and lizards. Another common rainforest plant is the strangler fig. It gradually grows up round a tree until the tree is suffocated and dies.

All about epiphytes

A lot of rainforest plants are epiphytes, which means they dangle their roots in the air to get the water and nutrients they need. They grow on the branches and trunks of the forest trees. Their seeds are dropped there by passing animals, or blown there on the breeze.

Tropical orchids are types of epiphyte. There are thousands of different kinds, some of them so rare they are worth a fortune to plant hunters.

Bromeliads are rainforest epiphytes, too. They have thick waxy leaves that make a bowl shape to collect rainwater for the plant to use. These little rainwater pools in turn provide a home for animals, such as frogs.

Useful ropes

Lianas can grow to more than 900 m (3,000 ft) long. They hang between trees, helping to hold the trees up. Lianas begin life as seedlings on the forest floor, which attach themselves to small trees. As the tree grows, so does the liana. Animals such as monkeys use lianas to climb trees and travel around in the forest canopy.

An Asian type of liana is called rattan. It is used to make baskets and furniture.

Fungi: small but vital

The tiniest plants in the rainforest are the most vital. Fungi and similar small plants send their roots into dead leaves and bark and help to rot them down quickly, releasing nutrients into the rainforest soil.

How to tap rubber

Natural rubber is a useful rainforest plant product that can be collected without damaging the trees. To do this, rubber collectors cut carefully into the bark of a rubber tree. Beads of white creamy latex, the raw ingredient of rubber, seep out and dribble down into buckets via a channel cut in the side of the tree. Once heated in vats over fires, the sap becomes stretchy and is ready for sale to a rubber company. Collecting rubber this way is called "rubber-tapping".

15

Trees in danger

A rainforest tree can take more than a hundred years to grow but only a few minutes to cut down. The large-scale cutting down of forests is called "deforestation".

Logging

Rainforest wood is called "hardwood" because it is tough and hard-wearing. People pay a lot of money for it. Hardwood is used to make products such as furniture and packing cases.

This factory in the Philippines produces elaborate carved furniture using wood from tropical forests.

Unfortunately, the most valuable hardwood trees grow alongside many less useful species. When a logging company cuts down one profitable tree, it may destroy dozens of other trees, leaving them to rot. To find enough useful trees, loggers can end up cutting down many hectares of forest.

On a smaller scale, local people cut down trees to burn as fuel. Many people who live in rainforest regions are very poor and cannot afford to buy fuel. They can only get it by collecting it for free in the forest.

Farming

Most of the world's rainforests are in countries that have overcrowded cities and many poor people. To find free land to farm, people often follow the roads cut into the rainforests by loggers. Then they cut down the forest to grow food for themselves and their families. But rainforest soil is very thin, and once the trees are gone it is soon washed away by the rain. It quickly becomes useless for growing anything and the settlers move on to cut down another area of forest.

Larger areas of deforestation are caused by commercial farming companies who clear land to make big plantations for profitable crops such as coffee, or to plant grass for cattle-grazing. The only way to keep the land fertile is for the farming companies to cover it regularly with lots of chemical fertilizer. Unfortunately this fertilizer often washes into local streams and rivers, contaminating the water.

PROFIT OR LOSS?

Mining, oil-drilling and damming are big business in rainforest regions.

A dam blocks a river, creating a giant reservoir of water behind it. The water is channelled through the dam to turn turbines that generate electricity. When the dam is built the reservoir floods a large area of forest.

To save time and money, the rainforest trees are sometimes left standing as a dam is built. Then the area is simply flooded, killing all the wildlife. "Scuba lumberjacks" then fell the trees underwater using diving equipment, and they float to the surface to be taken away. If they were left in the reservoir they would gradually rot and turn the water into acid that would pollute the water.

Big rainforest projects such as mines, oil wells and dams are very controversial. Organizations that try to protect the environment point out that the profit these schemes appear to make does not take into account the cost of the damage they do.

A section of Amazon rainforest clear-cut for a dam project.

People in danger

The rainforests of the world are home to "indigenous" peoples who have lived there for many centuries. As the forests are destroyed, their way of life is in grave danger.

Life in the Amazon region

Amazonian Indians hunt for food in the forest and grow crops on agricultural plots. They clear a small area of forest to grow crops, which are carefully chosen and varied from year to year so as not to use up all the soil's nutrients. After a while the Indians will move to another plot, leaving the forest to regrow, and causing the least possible impact on the natural life of the rainforest.

They also gather wild rainforest plants, which they use to make all kinds of useful things such as food, medicine, dyes, soap, clothing fibres and even insect repellent. There are thought to be several Amazon tribes living so deep in the forest they are not known to any outsiders.

Life in Africa

The Efe people make their home in the rainforests of Central Africa. They don't farm, but rely on the rainforest for their food. They hunt monkeys, birds and rodents and collect food such as honey, nuts and edible insects. When they hunt for honey they use special whistles to make a noise to lure the bees away from their nests.

The tribe owns few possessions – just a few baskets, bows and arrows and some simple homemade musical instruments. The African forests are being cleared so the tribe's way of life is in great danger. In addition to this threat, the Efe people live in war zones: many have been killed in the fighting.

Life in other rainforests

The rainforest tribes of Papua New Guinea in Australasia and those of Borneo in Malaysia hunt and grow food, too. They were once fierce headhunters, who shrank the heads of their enemies and displayed them in their villages as proof of their bravery. Now they battle against climate change, rainforest destruction and water pollution caused by careless mining and oil production.

A TOUGH FIGHT

When rainforest tribes first met people from outside, catastrophe quickly followed. They had no natural immunity from the diseases carried by outsiders, and many thousands died from everyday European diseases, such as chicken-pox and the common cold.

Now there is a further threat to the existence of rainforest peoples. As loggers, miners and settlers gradually move into rainforest regions, they often use violence to drive out the Indians.

Rainforest tribes are not rich and have little political influence. They find it hard to resist the destruction of their way of life.

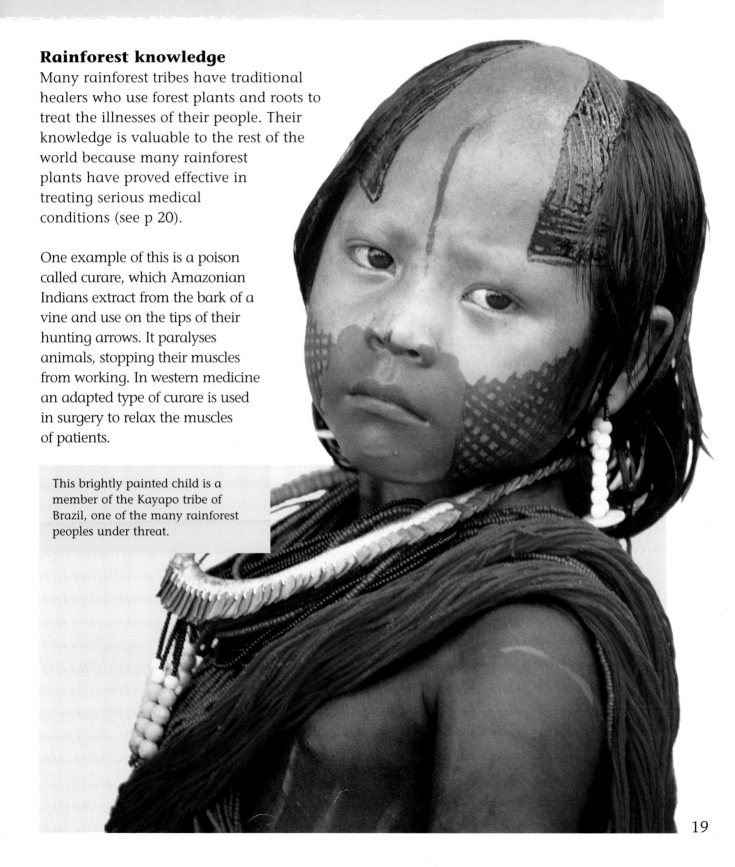

Rainforest knowledge

Many rainforest tribes have traditional healers who use forest plants and roots to treat the illnesses of their people. Their knowledge is valuable to the rest of the world because many rainforest plants have proved effective in treating serious medical conditions (see p 20).

One example of this is a poison called curare, which Amazonian Indians extract from the bark of a vine and use on the tips of their hunting arrows. It paralyses animals, stopping their muscles from working. In western medicine an adapted type of curare is used in surgery to relax the muscles of patients.

This brightly painted child is a member of the Kayapo tribe of Brazil, one of the many rainforest peoples under threat.

Saving rainforest plants

It could be that the true wealth of rainforests will be found not through selling the trees for timber or mining the ground, but through harvesting rainforest plants for medicine and food.

Good rainforest business

Crops which are harvested but then re-grow easily are called "sustainable". Sustainable rainforest crops include fruits, nuts, plant oils and some species of tree. It has been calculated that an area of rainforest that is carefully looked after and harvested sustainably earns a lot more money over the long term than if it were cut down and sold as wood.

The world's plant store

Many foods we eat were originally discovered in the rainforests. Mangoes, bananas, spices, coffee, chocolate and vanilla are all examples. Nowadays these are mainly grown on big plantations, but the rainforests still house a store of different varieties which can be used to help keep plantation crops healthy. By crossing old plant varieties with newly discovered ones, farmers can produce new types of crop with in-built protection against diseases and weather damage.

It's likely there are lots of foods still to be discovered in the rainforest. For instance, it's estimated there might be over 3,000 different kinds of rainforest fruits, yet so far we only know about a few of them.

The healing forest

At the moment 25% of all western medicines contain substances that originated in the rainforest. Yet only 1% of rainforest plants have so far been tested for medical use! It's possible that there are cures still to be found for many major illnesses.

Rainforest trees and plants produce an astonishing variety of fruits and seeds.

SAVING THE SEEDS

The rainforests are like a giant library of plant species. Botanists are trying to catalogue this library and collect seed samples before it is destroyed. They go on field trips to the forest to collect seeds, which they take back to "seed banks", run in the world's plant-studying centres. Here the seeds are identified, cleaned, x-rayed to see inside them and then dried and frozen. They can be preserved this way for hundreds of years and will still grow again if planted. That means they could be re-introduced into the wild in the future.

To help identify the seeds, the botanists bring home leaf samples, too. Kew Gardens in London has a seed bank and more than 7 million pressed leaf samples to help them name the seeds they collect.

A scientist at a seed bank in Malaysia works on a conservation programme for wild garlic.

Many pharmaceutical companies are now sending botanists (people who study plants) to rainforest regions to discover new useful plants. They talk to local healers to find out what they use plants for. Then they collect samples and take them home for analysis and testing in laboratories, to make certain that they are safe for human use. Rainforest plants are particularly rich in substances called alkaloids, which help protect them from disease and insect attack. Alkaloids make very effective human medicines, too.

Saving rainforest animals

Many rainforest creatures are in danger of extinction, but the more we know about them the more likely it is that we can find ways to save them. Here are some examples of how scientists are trying to help.

Last chance for orang-utans

Orang-utans are intelligent, gentle creatures, and the only apes that live in trees. Their natural home is on the Asian islands of Borneo and Sumatra, where the rainforest is fast disappearing and where the apes are illegally hunted. Now the orang-utan species is dying out.

By observing wild orang-utans and studying their habits, scientists can work out how many there are left, and how best to protect them. For instance, they have discovered that orang-utans can be moved to new areas of replanted forest, away from human settlements, if the right fruit trees are planted as food for them. The seeds of the orang-utans' favourite fruits have been collected from their droppings and planted in these new areas to grow.

Conservationists visit street markets and animal dealers to rescue baby orang-utans taken from the wild. The animals are often very sick by this point and they must be nursed back to health. They are taken to sanctuaries, where experts on orang-utan behaviour teach them the skills they need to survive, such as building nests and finding food. These are lessons their mothers would have taught them.

Gradually the orang-utans are encouraged to go out into the forest, and eventually to live permanently back in the wild.

Baby orang-utans are taken from their mothers and are sold as pets. The mother is killed in the process.

Scientists fit a sedated tiger with a radio collar.

Big cat rescue

Big cats, especially tigers, are highly endangered rainforest animals. One way to check on them is for scientists to sedate them with tranquillizer darts and fit them with radio collars. The tigers can then be tracked to find out where they roam. By doing this, scientists have discovered that when forest is cut down big cats are often left stranded in small remaining patches, unable to find mates or sufficient food. If this occurs they tend to stray into human settlements, where they are a danger and have to be shot.

One way scientists hope to save big cats is to establish "green corridors", which are protected natural routes between different patches of rainforest. In Central America biologists are hoping one day to create a "Panther Path" across countries to help save the jaguar. To plan for this they are tracking jaguars using radio collars, and have set up cameras on likely jaguar paths to check whether the cats use them.

Changing minds

Many rainforest creatures are illegally kidnapped or hunted every year. Tigers are illegally killed so that parts of their bodies can be used in traditional Chinese medicine. Their bones, eyes, whiskers and teeth are ground into pills and potions, which are thought to give people the animal's strength.

It is very hard to completely stamp out profitable criminal activity, but one way is to encourage local people to use their knowledge to save animals, not hunt them. Local wildlife rangers are good at explaining about their work to their own communities.

23

Saving rainforest trees

How can we save the rainforest trees, or try to replace them if they are lost? Here are some methods that are being tried.

Replanting or controlled logging

Planting new trees does not recreate an old rainforest as it once was, but it does help to stop the soil being washed away. When botanists replant they try to use tree species that have roots that will quickly spread out and help to anchor the soil before it disappears.

Another way to try to preserve the forest is to encourage new settlers to farm more like the native people, planting the right crops and moving their farm plots around so as not to exhaust the soil forever.

Sometimes forests have controlled logging, which means that the loggers are allowed to cut small groups or strips of trees down instead of large areas. That way a forest has more chance of surviving in the long run.

Rainforest tourism

Rainforest countries can make a good income by opening rainforest reserves to tourists. This is called "ecotourism". Many people are prepared to pay to visit such a beautiful plant- and animal-rich environment. National parks have been created by law in some rainforest areas. They are managed by governments to ensure that they are not destroyed.

Rainforest law

There are now international laws that outlaw the cutting down of endangered rainforests, the stealing of land from native people and the poaching of rare animals. It is very hard to enforce these laws because rainforests are usually in isolated, difficult-to-guard areas. In addition, they are often in the world's poorest countries, places that badly need to earn the money they can get from selling their wood. These countries often have big international debts,

BRAZIL NUT SCIENCE

Brazil nuts are a very valuable crop. They earn over $40 million every year for South America. But brazil nut trees can't be grown in plantations. They will only grow and produce nuts in remote undisturbed rainforest, surrounded by different tree species. The nuts are collected by local people, called *castanas*, who hunt for the best crops.

Biologists have been studying brazil nut trees in the Upper Amazon, to try to find out as much as they can about them. If they find ways to get a better harvest, they hope to persuade people that there is more money to be made from brazil-nut collecting than chopping forests down. Researchers studied 1,000 trees, counting every pod that fell. They opened lots of nuts, fitted a tiny magnetic strip inside each one and closed them up again. Then they discovered that rodents called agoutis ate or buried the nuts around the forest, helping to spread the tree to new areas. The biologists used a magnetic detector to find the buried nuts and record where new trees were likely to grow.

money they have borrowed from international banks and must repay. Politicians, people in business and environmentalists argue over the ways to solve the threat to the rainforest, but there are some things that everyone can do to help. You can find out more on page 28.

A worker collects Brazil nuts. The nuts are located inside the grapefruit-sized pods.

Collecting knowledge

The more we know about the rainforests and what is happening to them, the more we can help save them. Here are some of the methods used to collect information.

Satellite images

We know that rainforests are disappearing because satellites are able to monitor them from space using instruments that gather information about the Earth's surface. Satellites designed for this kind of work carry sensing equipment that can detect different types of radiation. Everything on the surface of the Earth sends out or reflects some radiation, but different objects send out different amounts. Satellites measure

Satellite images help scientists to keep track of rainforest destruction and regeneration. In this picture, the light-coloured areas are land that has been cleared.

this and transmit the data back to Earth, where computers process it to make images that show features of the landscape in different colours.

Satellite images are detailed enough to show small-scale logging, farming, roads and forest fires. Their sensitive measuring equipment can even be used to distinguish between different tree sizes and species.

Preventing disturbance

Scientists who study the lives of tribal people are called anthropologists. Many work in rainforest areas, talking to local people and recording details of their lives.

Deep in the Amazon rainforest there are thought to be around 17 tribes who have not yet encountered outsiders. Many anthropologists believe it is better to leave them undisturbed, because once they meet outside people they are likely to die quickly of diseases that are unknown to them, such as the common cold. But these people are at great risk from illegal loggers and settlers arriving to take their land.

Researchers are trying to find traces of where these tribes live – while avoiding meeting them – in the hope that laws can be passed to protect their land and leave them undisturbed.

Gene banks – the last chance

Scientists are trying to save threatened rainforest animals and plants by collecting samples of each species and trying to keep them alive for the future. These samples are known as "gene banks".

Some highly endangered rainforest animals now have such low populations that the only way to keep their species alive is to breed them in zoos. In the near future the only tigers and orang-utans left in the world may be the ones in zoos.

One day it could be possible to use genetic science to produce more of these animals by cloning, but it's not yet certain whether that will be possible – at the moment the science of cloning is in its infancy. Sadly, it's too late for many rainforest species that have already disappeared from our world.

RAINFOREST CRIMEBUSTING

Rare rainforest animal smuggling makes big money. It's estimated that up to 12 million Brazilian wild animals may be bought and sold illegally every year. Out of every ten animals captured only one survives to reach its destination, usually as an exotic pet. The rarest creatures make the most money. A blue macaw parrot might sell for US $25,000 and an endangered tamarin monkey for US $20,000.

Customs police try to investigate the criminal gangs who carry on this practice, and find out who buys the animals from the gangs. The police may talk to contacts and hunt around local markets in rainforest areas, or run investigations on pet shops and websites in the USA, Europe and Asia. If possible, they try to rescue the animals and return them to the wild.

What can you do?

Here are some suggestions for ways that you can find out more about the rainforests of the world and help to stop their destruction.

Watch what you buy

Try to avoid buying things made of tropical hardwoods. That way you will be helping to reduce the number of trees cut down. The main types of wood to avoid are mahogany, teak and rosewood.

It's hard to find out exactly where products come from and how they have been produced, but look carefully for any information on the packaging. Look out for the words "sustainable source", which means the harvesting of the crops is being properly managed to try to preserve the environment.

Cattle-farming in rainforest areas has led to deforestation because the land is cleared for grazing. It's estimated that for each beefburger produced from cattle grazed on cleared land, over 5 sq m (55 sq ft) of forest has been destroyed. Try to make sure you know where the meat you eat comes from. Ask in restaurants or write to food companies to find out the facts.

When your family goes shopping, suggest everyone tries to buy goods produced by companies that are committed to saving endangered environments. Look out for fair trade products, too. When you buy these items, a fair amount of money goes back to the farmers who originally grew the crop. You can buy fair trade coffee, chocolate and bananas from rainforest regions.

Recycle your stuff

Try to use recycled paper when you can, and make sure you recycle the paper that you no longer need. In the long run it will help to reduce the number of trees being cut down.

Recycling uses less industrial energy than making a new product, and helps to cut down global warming. Find out how you can recycle your tin cans, bottles and cardboard, as well as paper.

You could make some posters encouraging your family and your classmates to recycle things.

Don't buy exotic animals

Don't buy rainforest animals as pets. You will only be encouraging criminals to catch more of them for profit. The animals are better off in the wild.

Get involved

There are lots of schemes run by recognized conservation charities that involve children and school classes in conservation projects. For instance, you might want to help save an orang-utan or a tiger. Ask your teacher if your class could become involved with a conservation charity.

Here are some useful website addresses to help you start:

www.rainforestweb.org

Go to this address for a great list of rainforest sites for young people. It will link you to them.

www.panda.org

The website of the Worldwide Fund for Nature. Find out more about their international work.

www.tropical-forests.com

Maps, facts and projects for you to try.

www.rainforestlive.org.uk

Learn about rainforest expeditions and research and try out some games, too.

www.zoomschool.com

Go to the rainforest section of this online kids' school.

www.eduweb.com

Go to the Amazon section of this site for rainforest facts and games.

www.kidsplanet.org

Animated activities and facts.

www.pbs.org/journeyinto amazonia/

Travel into the Amazon rainforest

www.nationalgeographic.com

All sorts of rainforest information, including a virtual tour of a rainforest at night.

Glossary

Alkaloid
A natural substance that protects plants from disease and insect attack.

Anthropologist
Someone who studies the lifestyles and customs of people.

Biodiversity
The wide variety of living things on the Earth.

Botanist
Someone who studies plants.

Bromeliad
A rainforest plant with thick waxy leaves that grow in a bowl-shape.

Buttress root
Tree root that grows above the ground, to help the tree stand firm.

Canopy
A thick layer of leaves and branches high up in the rainforest trees.

Carbon dioxide
A gas, also called CO_2, that is released when fuel, such as wood and coal, burns. It is also breathed out by animals in respiration and absorbed by plants in the process of photosynthesis.

Climate
The weather and temperature usually found in an area.

Cloud forest
A forest that gets the moisture it needs from mist rather than rain.

Deforestation
The destruction of trees over large areas.

Ecosystem
A natural system, also called a web of life, that includes all the living things in a particular area.

Ecotourism
Tourism aimed at benefiting local environments, not damaging them.

Emergent tree
Very tall rainforest tree that towers above the others around it.

Environment
The world around us.

Epiphyte
Plant that dangles its roots in the air to get the water it needs.

Equatorial rainforest
A rainforest that grows near the Equator, the area that stretches around the middle of the Earth. Here the climate is always warm.

Fungi
Tiny plants that do not photosynthesize, but instead get the food they need from dead leaves and rotting bark.

Gene bank
A collection of endangered plants and animals kept in captivity to help preserve their species, possibly by using genetic science in the future.

Global warming
The possible warming of the world's climate because of too much CO_2 in the atmosphere.

Hardwood
The tough hard-wearing timber from rainforest trees, such as mahogany, rosewood and teak.

Humidity
Warm, damp air.

Indigenous
A living thing that belongs naturally to an area.

Leaf litter
A layer of rotting leaves on the floor of a forest.

Liana
Rope-like plants that grow up trees.

Mangrove
A kind of rainforest tree that stands high on stilt-like roots and can live in salt-water swamps.

Nutrients
Minerals that plants take from the soil to help them grow.

Overstorey
The very top layer of the rainforest.

Photosynthesis
The process by which green plants take in sunlight, CO_2 and water to make oxygen and food.

Plantation
A large farmed area of one crop, such as coffee.

Primary forest
Forest that has never been cut down.

Recycling
Turning waste into something that is reusable.

Secondary forest
Forest which grows back after primary forest has been cut down.

Seed bank
A store of seeds kept in frozen conditions to preserve them for study and future use.

Sustainable crop
A crop that can re-grow after it is harvested.

Temperate rainforest
A rainforest that grows in a part of the world where there are cool seasons as well as warm ones.

Understorey
The area between the ground and the thickest layer of leaves (the canopy) of a rainforest.

Index